12 Secrets
Luxury Home Sellers Know
That You Can Use Today

Jack Cotton

For John R. Alger, Esq.
Mentor, Confidant and Friend

Acknowledgments

Writing books turned out to be significantly more work than I had imagined. Without the help of some very talented experts as well as the love and support of family and friends, it would be so much easier to toss the project aside and take some time off.

Norma Jean Lutz was immensely helpful in getting the first draft completed. Her real estate experience resulted in some great questions that shaped the outcome of this work.

Susan Kendrick of Write To Your Market (www.writetoyourmarket.com) spent hours with me on the phone and via email to hone the title and subtitle.

Even after untold hours of writing, rewriting, and polishing, I am amazed at how Barbara McNichol (www.BarbaraMcNichol.com) takes the manuscript further, adding even more questions and suggestions for deeper exploration of various thoughts as she edits.

Joseph Dobrian (www.JosephDobrian.com) helped with the final polishing of the manuscript. He gave me several pointers on saying more with less and brought the book to the next level.

Even with years of practice, I still cannot type as fast as the thoughts pour out. As a result, much of this book was dictated electronically. Keith at eWord Solutions (www.eWordSolutions.com) transcribes and turns around near-perfect Word documents, usually the next day.

I am an objective person and think this book cover is clean, elegant, and riveting. Thanks to Andrew Newman (www.newmandesign.com) for his patience and diligence as we went through dozens of evolutions to arrive at the final version.

Lastly, I want to express my gratitude for the love and support of my family, including my four kids—Melissa, Andrew, Maxwell, and Alexa—and most of all, my supportive wife, Ann Marie. Aside from being a great proofreader and sounding board, whenever she hears one of my ideas for a new project, she always says, "You can do that."

Introduction

I started my real estate career in 1974 at the height of one of the worst real estate and economic crises in our country. Interest rates were in double digits, people had to wait in line to get gasoline on odd and even days, and economic activity had nearly ground to a halt.

Between then and now, I've had the opportunity to work with thousands of people who bought and sold real estate. I've learned much from all of my clients, but specifically I learned many powerful secrets from luxury homeowners as I worked with them to sell their properties. I've also gained valuable insights into the mistakes people might make when selling real estate.

A few of the high-end people I've been privileged to work with fit the profile of the millionaire that Dr. Thomas Stanley described in his stellar book, The Millionaire Next Door. That brand of millionaire consists of conservative, hard-working people who live well within their means and have managed to save and accumulate a net worth of more than a million dollars over their careers. This could describe people in your neighborhood whom you never knew were millionaires.

At the opposite end of the wealth spectrum are those who've worked hard, founded companies, and sold them for several hundred million dollars—sometimes even more than once.

Then at both ends of the spectrum can be found individuals who came into money suddenly through inheritance, lottery winnings, or other means. While you might love to be in this situation, what can be learned from guessing the right number or being born to well-off parents?

In this book, you'll learn from those who made their money the old-fashioned way: they earned it. Their "good luck" came through working and recognizing opportunity. This kind of luck provides secrets you can learn from; it's different from the "pure chance" kind of luck, which is akin to waiting for lightning to strike.

While luxury homeowners may on occasion buy a lottery ticket, they don't depend on that ticket to create a path toward lasting wealth. Instead, they achieve their goals by working a plan. And along the way, they can teach others their secrets—as this book reveals.

During the course of my career, I've worked mostly in high-end real estate with people who own second, third, or retirement homes valued well into seven and eight figures. I've always found it fascinating to witness how they approach selling their homes compared to how the not-as-wealthy undertake this process.

Mostly, my clients have arrived at a position and time in life when they can afford a luxury home through hard work, intelligence, and being at the right place at the right time. They now make the kind of money that allows them to own a $4 million second home, for example. When they wish to sell that home, how do they approach the entire process so it produces better results than most people would be able to achieve?

In thinking about answers to that question, I developed 12 critical secrets for anyone who's considering selling their home your. Applying these secrets will help you maximize your experience and avoid common mistakes.

As does my companion book 12 Secrets Luxury Home Buyers Know That You Can Use Today, this book offers you a "best practices" list from luxury home sellers. I'm not saying that all luxury home sellers use all 12 secrets consistently. Some actually do choose a golfing buddy to sell their multimillion-dollar estates, instead of hiring the most qualified agents.

Through the 12 secrets in this book, you'll explore how to prepare mentally for selling your home, then address ways to prepare the property itself. You'll find a checklist to follow as you look over its exterior as well as its interior—including the basement pipes—to make sure your house is presented in the best possible light to a potential buyer.

What about the dilemma of finding and selecting a real estate agent? From the gazillion real estate agents in your own neighborhood, you'll discover which ones to interview and how to prevent wasting time in selecting the right one. You'll learn how to ask the right questions and how to hire the agent for the right reasons.

What about pricing? The luxury home seller wants to get the highest price the market can support, in the shortest amount of time, with the least amount of aggravation to his or her family. I often see sellers set a price for the wrong reasons. If you plan to sell your home to solve financial problems, you could run the risk of pricing it in a way that attracts the wrong kind of potential buyers.

For example, if your property is priced too high (e.g., $500,000 when it should be $400,000), potential buyers looking in the $500,000 category will be disappointed when they see what your house doesn't have. Meanwhile, prospects in the $400,000 price range won't even look at your home because they've instantly rejected it based on your unrealistic value proposition. This pricing example reveals just one of the secrets luxury home sellers use.

While the title of this book suggests lessons like this are secrets, they aren't really secret at all. In fact, most are common-sense strategies that people know but simply fail to implement. (I guess that means they might as well be secrets, and that is why I label them so.)

Please read this book and come away with the secrets (common-sense strategies) you can put into action immediately. To assist you, I've ended each "Secret" segment with action steps.

Make these secrets your own and reap the rewards of faster, smoother, more profitable selling.

12 Secrets
Luxury Home Sellers Know That You Can Use Today

Table of Contents

LUXURY HOME SELLERS KNOW:

Secret #1: Luxury Home Sellers Are All Business

Throughout the selling process, owners of seven-figure luxury homes maintain an attitude akin to embarking on a business venture—that is, they attach little, if any, emotion to the experience. They've learned to detach their personal feelings from the transaction itself. They're mentally prepared for a solid business exchange.

Changing Your Lifestyle

Easier said than done, you might argue. After all, when you put your own home on the market to sell, you inevitably face a change of lifestyle. You have become a visitor in your own home—and need to shift your mindset accordingly.

Even though this is the home you've been living in for years—perhaps even decades—it now must be presented so others will feel comfortable when they come to visit: so comfortable they'll want to buy it.

That means dirty clothes must be picked up, beds made, countertops cleared off, clutter dispensed with. In effect, you're preparing for company at a moment's notice, but it's not Uncle Charlie or Aunt Jane who are stopping by. They're people you don't know, but you must put on your best face for them.

You never know when this company will arrive. You never know if they'll be wearing a white glove to check for dust atop your doorframes. You never know if they'll spend an hour or only five minutes.

This "not knowing" has the potential for causing you stress. Family members who have not prepared for this lifestyle disruption may become frustrated and discouraged. It can easily happen.

Prepare for Feelings of Rejection

Often, I see sellers look at their own homes through their hearts, not their eyes. Their thoughts (subconscious though they may be) run something like this: "This is my house. We've lived in this house for twenty years. This is the greatest house in the whole neighborhood if not the entire universe. Certainly *anyone* can see that. The second they walk through the doorway, they'll feel the same way I do and want to own it."

Soon enough, the shocking truth comes up. Everyone does *not* like this house. Potential buyers see your home through their *eyes*, not their hearts. Hence, sellers must deal with the nasty feelings of rejection.

You know about rejection, right? Think back to your first high school dance, lights turned low, maple gymnasium floors polished to a high sheen. Streamers hung from the overhead lights, music filled the space. Suddenly that great song blared out of the speakers. You *loved* that song. You knew the time was right. You made your way across the room to ask that special person to dance. But when you did, you heard a resounding "no thanks" or worse "get lost!" That pierced your heart. And that feeling of rejection from those formative years stuck with you—forever.

I've seen it happen again and again. A client's house goes on the market. After a prospective buyer walks through to look, the seller hears that resounding "no thanks." From the seller's resulting distress, I can guess that the rejection is triggering past events. He or she may be subconsciously harkening back to the night of the dance in the high school gym (or a similar experience). Rejected again.

If prospect after prospect says "no," you, too, might live through another lifetime of difficult feelings.

Face the Truth

The key to approaching the selling process like a seasoned luxury home seller, then, is to face and accept this truth: *Not everyone will like your house.* It simply will not appeal to every person who looks at it, for any number of reasons, many of which you'll never know.

Have faith. *Someone* out there wants, needs, and likes the beautiful house you're offering. It's your job to concentrate on that fact. It's your job to keep the premises in a ready-to-show condition. It's your job to remember that, while you're emotionally attached to this property, your prospects are not. Ultimately, it's your job to keep your attitude clear of the tricky emotions that could slow down the process.

Take a cue from luxury home sellers and learn to reassess your mindset and your emotions. Before long, you'll view this sale as a business transaction and *only* a business transaction.

Action Steps for Secret #1

Think back to a time when you faced rejection. How did you handle it? Then make a commitment to yourself to re-frame this rejection: You as a person were not rejected; an idea or proposition was rejected.

Put your emotional attachment to your house in the closet. Refuse to feel rejected when those who come to look say "no thanks." Learn to use the magic word of the luxury home seller: NEXT!

Secret #2: Luxury Home Sellers Use Experts

Although people debate whether it's necessary to contract with a real estate agent when selling their homes, a luxury home seller weighs in with an unequivocal "yes."

Dealing with the Experts

Wealthy people are used to dealing with experts in all aspects of their lives. When they have medical, legal, or tax questions or needs, they have the ability to obtain—and they therefore expect—the best guidance and expertise available. Many times, this is a point of honor for them.

On the other hand, I see sellers who view a real estate agent as a toll-taker on the road to selling their property. To this kind of seller, the agent takes a piece off the top but doesn't intrinsically add value to the selling process.

People who have that perception are likely to hire agents for all the wrong reasons—like hiring the one who promises the highest home price during the listing presentation or who is a next-door neighbor, relative, or golfing buddy.

In contrast, sellers of luxury homes have the opposite viewpoint. They know that the right agent, armed with a proper marketing plan, will bring value and help them realize the highest end of their price range. (More about what "price range" refers to in Secret #3.) They view their real estate agent as an essential advisor—just as important as the other professionals in their lives.

They love to know that their orthopedist treats the top performers on the local sports team or that their attorney is the one who wrote the law on a given subject. They will accept nothing less than the most expert practitioners in any field.

Selecting the Right Real Estate Agent

The question then becomes: How do luxury home sellers find the experts they want to hire? And how do they know these people are accomplished in their fields?

The answer: They ask for recommendations from their friends and associates and then conduct online and local research to augment recommendations from these sources. Most important, they conduct a powerful interview with the recommended expert, either on the phone or in person.

This lesson was reinforced recently during my experience with the executor of an estate, and his siblings, who were selling their family's multimillion-dollar home from long distance.

Determined to choose the best local real estate agent for the task, this family set up an organized and systematic process of preliminary telephone calls and interviews. The head decision-maker for the family began by calling real estate offices at random while the rest of the family listened in. On each call, he requested to speak with the office manager and asked, "Who would be the best agent in your firm to market our ocean front property?" Then he listed all the qualifications of the agent he wanted to work with.

What happened? Some managers never called him back; other managers were too busy to even talk to him and didn't take the call. Still others were just rude.

After calling every company in town, the family narrowed the field to three agents. Then their spokesman invited each of them to sit in front of family members, make a presentation, and answer questions. My company was one of three chosen to do the interview—and we were hired.

When the listing agreement was signed, I asked this client how the family decided on this process for selecting a real estate agent. He told me their father had started his business modestly and built it into a hugely successful company. Their father often said the cornerstone of his success was his ability to interview and choose great people for critical roles in the firm. In turn, the family members believed that, in selling the property their deceased father left, they should adhere to a structured truth-finding process to find the right agent to sell it. Many luxury home sellers follow a similar process even without the family history that this family had.

Ask the Right Questions

People I've dealt with over the years have used different variations of this process, but the common thread is this: They're used to dealing with experts who have set procedures about how they work. They want to see a presentation. They compile a list of questions. How questions are answered tells them whether the person they're talking to is right for the job.

Make the Process Yours

If you're an ordinary home seller (as opposed to a high-end seller), can you do the same thing? Absolutely you can. All it takes is a little knowledge and understanding of the process.

Let's say you've already ascertained the need for hiring an agent. You've decided that you should view this person as a highly valued team member who will contribute to the successful sale of your property.

First, be sure to make the time, and put in the effort, to interview at least two or three agents until you find one with whom you feel comfortable. Maybe you like someone who is pushy and opinionated. On the other hand, maybe you prefer someone whose manner is laid-back and who acts as a counselor to you. The ideal selection may be somewhere in the middle. The important thing is to pick the style that's right for you.

Remember: In the course of the selling process, your property will likely be shown to many people. During that period, you'll be spending a great deal of time with this agent. So, make sure you're on the same wavelength and that the agent listens to your concerns.

Use this helpful list of questions to ask agents before selecting the best one for you:

- **How long have you been in business?** While the amount of time the agent has been in the real estate business is no guarantee of success, you do want to assess the experience of that agent.

- **What professional organizations do you belong to?** Membership in the National Association of Realtors and its various Councils shows that your agent has made a commitment to the professional community, and keeps up with changes in the real estate industry.

- **May I have a copy of your résumé?** Engaging a real estate agent to sell your home is like hiring a person to work for you. Would you conduct a job interview with someone who doesn't have a résumé? Do you want to hire an agent who doesn't have enough pride in his or her qualifications and experience to submit them to you in writing?

- **How many hours a week do you spend previewing listings?** You want to know that your agent has a finger on the pulse of the real estate scene in your area, and will inspect new offerings as soon as they enter the market.

- **What support staff do you have? Will I be talking with them or with you?** The agent you hire should spend as much time as possible finding prospects and showing your property. Filling out forms, writing ads, and chasing paperwork may be necessary chores, but it robs time from your house being shown or an open house being conducted.

Who will actually be showing my home to prospective buyers?

Some agents are great at making listing presentations—and then they're never seen again because an assistant does all the property showings. If this is the case, make sure you meet this assistant. I have met lots of sellers who aren't happy with the caliber of the person showing their home after they'd signed on with the local "high-powered" agent.

This is also a good time to find out if accompanied showings are customary in your area. In some locales, agents install a lock box, and cooperating agents from the Multiple Listing Service (MLS) call the seller directly and then show the property without the listing agent being present. While this may be common practice, make sure you feel comfortable with it and/or lay out your own rules for making appointments.

- **How are you different from other agents in the area?** Real estate agents offer different levels of service. Ask your agent what makes him or her different from the pack. What can he or she offer that others cannot?
- **May I have a copy of your listing contract?** When you get it, you want to ask: What is the duration of the listing agreement? Does the agent and/or company guarantee the work with a cancellation provision? If so, read it carefully. Know your rights, what's expected of you, and what you can expect from the agent and/or company. Most important, find out the duration of the contract and how you might get out of it early. Also find out any obligations you have should the contract expire or be canceled by either party.

May I have a copy of your marketing plan?

You'll find information about marketing in Secret 6, but know this first: You want to work with an agent who has a marketing plan and will customize it to the unique needs of you and your property. The plan should include details on traditional marketing and online marketing. Most important, it should include how the agent markets to other real estate agents in the area. Why? Because more than 50 percent of all home sales involve more than one real estate agent or company. Ask which MLS service your agent is a member of, and how quickly he or she submits listings to the service.

- **What professional designations have you earned?** Did you know that somewhere around 2,000,000 people in the United States have their real estate license? Of these, more than 1,000,000 belong to the National Association of REALTORS®, which means they are serious about and spend a significant amount of time in the business. Of all the REALTORS® in the country, only a small percentage hold the Certified Residential Specialist (CRS) or Accredited Buyer Representative (ABR) designations. Agents who either have or are working toward these designations tend to be the most professional and capable in the business. Note: There are countless other designations. Ask whether the agent you are interviewing has one, find out which one(s), and probe into how it would help in the sale of your home.

- **Can you explain your policy on agency to me? Do you only work with sellers?** During your listing appointment, your prospective real estate agent must explain agency laws to you and ask you to sign an agency disclosure form. As a seller, you need an agent who will represent you. The agent you select may also work with buyers. There is nothing wrong with this; you just need to know and acknowledge in writing that you know.

- **How can you stay in tune with inventory in this market?** Many (but not all) homes for sale are listed in the local MLS (Multiple Listing Service). Some homes, whether they are for sale by owners (FSBOs); foreclosures, or homes constructed on spec by builders may not be listed on the MLS. Ask how your agent plans to promote your particular property.

- **How quickly do you respond to emails?** Luxury home sellers can be the type of people who stand in front of a microwave and yell, "Hurry up!" They want replies in seconds. Most of all, they want to know what to expect. You, too, will want an agent who will be available when needed.

One Last Question

Let me relate another experience that led me to add one more question to this list.

I once worked with a high-end seller in her 80s who had beautiful blue eyes and always dressed in clothes that matched the shade. In the course of her lifetime, she and her husband had bought and sold more than a dozen homes around the country.

As I came to the close of my presentation, she said to me, "John, you've done a great job with the presentation. Now I'd like you to take me to the front door and show me my home as if I were the buyer." This woman's marvelous request becomes question #14.

Will you please take me to the front door and show me my home as if I were the buyer?

The caveat here is that you only need to have the agent show you two or three rooms to get a feel for how your home will be represented. This is a great way to find out if that agent has been listening to you during your interview.

Add Experts to Your Team

As you begin to sell your home, you'll need an attorney, lender, title company, and home inspector. Many of the sample questions here can be adapted to any of these professionals. Further, finding these experts will be the result of the same research you did to find your real estate agent. The only difference is that you can add the agent to your list of sources for referrals to experts.

Action Steps for Secret #2

Create a list of experts you'll need to sell your home. Consider including these professionals:

1. Real estate agents
2. Lenders
3. Attorneys
4. Title companies
5. Inspectors

Compose your lists of questions and modify them for each category of professional.

Secret #3: Luxury Home Sellers Know How to Price Their Property to Sell

One distinct difference I see in the way high-end sellers approach the sale of their properties compared to other sellers is that they know the importance of pricing their homes correctly. Pricing your home *incorrectly* often results in attracting the wrong prospects and possibly delaying or completely discouraging a sale.

Avoid Being Misguided

Many people who get ready to sell a house have the misguided perception that their house will sell for a certain price. No matter what happens, they *insist* it will sell for that amount, period. Therefore, it doesn't matter all that much to them what kind of expertise comes their way to help market it. Nor does it matter what kind of preparation they do to put their property on the market. (More about preparing for the sale later.)

This misguided thinking often leads them to engage the services of an agent based on the offering price suggested. In reality, *setting* a price and *getting* that price can be worlds apart.

To clearly understand pricing, realize that a range of values exist for every property. In my experience, the selling price can range somewhere between two and four percentage points. This is different from how most people think, which is there's only one carved-in-stone price for every property.

The test becomes whether your property sells at the low end of that range or the high end. The value a great agent brings to the sale of your home is achieving a price that's at the top end of that range.

Understand Market Value

High-end sellers typically know the markets; they understand the concept of market value. As a result, they price their houses according to market value.

People who don't understand market value tend to be more concerned with their present financial situation. For instance, they think about buying that new car or paying their son's or daughter's college tuition. To attempt to cover these costs, they add the required amount to the selling price of their house.

Sellers who do this should expect a rude awakening. The truth is, buyers don't care about a seller's financial situation. All they care about is this: Where does your property fit into the context of the current market? And how does it compare to similar offerings on the market?

As a seller, you want to set the highest price the market will support for your property. Believe me, that's not likely the amount that will solve all your financial problems. To get those extra funds, you can always buy a lottery ticket. Indeed, you have the same or better chance of hitting the lottery than selling an overpriced home—especially in the market that exists as this book is being written.

Set the Right Price Early

Once you have set the *right* price for your house in your marketplace, you have the best chance of getting the most qualified buyer prospects to visit it.

Let's say a seller plans to put on the market a house that should run close to $400,000. But because of pressing financial needs, the property goes up for sale at $500,000—just to see if it will actually bring in that much.

Here's what happens: The potential buyers looking in the $500,000 category walk through your house and feel disappointed with the lack of certain amenities—especially compared to the other $500,000 homes they've been looking at. Meanwhile, all the buying prospects in the $400,000 price range won't even look at your house because they've rejected your value proposition. That is, they've rejected your home because the price exceeds their price target.

What happens next? Because you've priced the home right out of the market, the wrong people will be looking at it—and consequently it could sit unsold for a long time.

Don't Count on Winning the Lottery

I'm not an avid buyer of lottery tickets. However, every once in a while, when the payoff amount in our area gets up to two or three hundred million dollars, I'll break down and buy a ticket. For a few minutes after I purchase that ticket, I fantasize about all the things I'll do if I win that money. Then those fantasies fade away as quickly as the morning mist, and I continue with the rest of my day.

I've noticed that many home sellers get that same lottery-winning feeling when they put their properties on the market. They fantasize about what they'll do when their properties sell: take that exotic vacation, buy a Rolex, pay that college tuition bill. Or they reflect on how they'll bail themselves out of the financial mess they're in.

Clearly, they're thinking about spending the sales proceeds—and so, they price the house accordingly. However, buyers don't care about financing a seller's dreams—and they won't.

Here's why. Imagine being a serious buyer who visits two houses in the same city. They both have four bedrooms, nice lots, plenty of privacy. In addition, they're both in perfect condition and located in the same general area of town.

Now imagine that one is priced at $400,000 and the other at $500,000. As an educated buyer, you might wonder why one virtually identical house is priced at $100,000 more. You can be almost certain that the seller has an agenda such as the following: He wants to bail out of his credit card debt, he's got a child entering college, and his family wants to move to an area where homes are more expensive. That's why he needs to get $100,000 more for his house.

Will you, the buyer, react by saying, "Well, of course I'd be glad to help you out and pay $100,000 more for that property"?

The luxury home seller knows that buyers decide on the price they're willing to pay based on competing offerings. Therefore, when you put your house on the market, take into consideration the pricing data for your area—which is exactly what luxury home sellers do—or you'll never sell.

Know That Asking and Getting Aren't the Same

Many times, sellers tell me they heard about a certain house that went on the market for a specific price. They want to use that price as the guideline for setting *their* price. That's when I gently remind them that *asking* a certain price and *getting* that price can be two different things.

Add to that the danger of your property staying on the market longer than it should. It can get a stigma attached to it like a burr. Instead of holding out for that fantasy price you'd dreamed of, you face lowering the price just to move it. Once that stigma takes hold, buyers may not consider your home again, no matter how much you lower the price.

Beware: Buyers Fear Rejection

In my experience, typical buyers in most markets don't like to offer more than 10 percent off the listed price of a home. They declare they don't want to insult a seller with a lower offer. Of course, exceptions to that rule occur in every market but generally, this 10 percent guideline holds true.

Let's look at this scenario. Even though a buyer says he doesn't want to insult the seller with a reduced offer, that's probably not the real reason. Think back to that high school dance. The buyer doesn't want to feel rejected by making an offer that's too low and having it turned down. He or she is afraid to make an emotional commitment that might not work out. How would he face his friends and family?

If the seller rejects that offer, the potential buyer experiences a huge stab of rejection right through the heart. I can assure you, buyers avoid this result at all cost by not making such a low offer in the first place.

Again, this is the inherent danger of overpricing.

Find Ways to Test the Price

The best way to test a selected sales price is to:

- Choose the best, most professional agent and ask for that expert's pricing recommendation.
- Understand the process the agent will use to arrive at the suggested offering price.

Ask your agent to bring in other agents from his or her company to render their opinion of the optimal offering price. In a perfect world, they would not be aware of the discussions you've had with your agent regarding price.

What's the ultimate test for your market price? The measure of market activity on your home. To obtain sales records, ask your agent for regular traffic reports from the local Multiple Listing Service (MLS) and Realtor.com, for example. Ideally, your agent is using websites that will generate traffic reports in addition to these.

If scores of agents look at your property online but no one calls to walk through the property, or if hundreds of people look at your property on Realtor.com and no one calls to see your house, take that as concrete proof that the market has rejected your value proposition.

I tell sellers that MLS and Realtor.com traffic *predict* the market's reaction to the price of your house like a barometer predicts the weather. Together, you and your agent should read these indicators to adjust the price to market levels.

Here's an example. Joan Witter, an agent in our company, recently sold one of her listings for $995,000. It had been on the market for two years at a higher price, with little activity.

After the sale closed, the buyer commented to Joan how much she had always wanted this house and had been looking at it online during the entire two years it sat on the market.

Not once did this buyer call to see the house. Not once did she call an agent for more information. She just watched anonymously and waited. When the price was adjusted to the "right" price of $995,000, she came in and paid full price.

When sellers say "the buyer can always make an offer," they forget that in order to get an offer, someone has to actually come and see the house. But if it's priced too high, no one comes and no one offers. It's really that simple.

What Has Recently Sold Nearby?

In any market, competing offerings make up an important part of the picture, but one must also look at recent sales of homes similar to yours. "Recent" is defined as being within the past six months. Knowing those numbers will help you determine whether the real estate market in your area is declining or rising.

If prices are going up, you wouldn't base your pricing decision on sales from six months ago, would you? At the same time, if prices are going down, you can't use prices that occurred six months ago either. They're no longer relevant in today's market.

So examine all the sales that have occurred within the past six months and adjust them for these factors:

1. Time. Market values go up and down over periods of time.
2. Usability. Compare the age and condition of the other offerings to yours.
3. Utility—Compare similar offerings in terms of square footage, design, number of bedrooms, and other factors.

By taking these steps, you'll be *more objective* and *less subjective* when pricing your home.

The luxury home seller knows that determining the initial and final offering price is probably the most important part of what your trusted, well-chosen expert real estate agent does for you. So put a mechanism in place to help you.

For my clients, I use Excel spreadsheets that track relevant sales data. Others use different methods; just be sure they have a way of assessing the sales occurring in the market to account for differences between other properties and your property.

For instance, perhaps one house sold for $400,000 on the south side of town. Your data indicate an average sale in that area demands 20 percent higher prices than in your side of town. You'd make an adjustment for that. Maybe another sale took place six months ago when prices were 10 percent higher. Similarly, you'd need to make an adjustment for that.

This is what you can ask your real estate agent to do for you. It's why you selected an expert to market your property in the first place. Ask your agent, "How did you arrive at your suggested offering price?" "Which price did you use and how did you adjust for the differences between the houses that have sold and the one I'm selling?" Then ask to see the data behind the logic and advice.

Get an Appraiser Involved

It's sometimes wise to order an appraisal by a certified appraiser when you first put your house on the market. This is especially true when market data are scant or your property has unusual characteristics. Agents have been known to solicit your listing by suggesting an artificially high offering price. That's why an appraisal by an expert with no vested interest in the value outcome serves you well when you're setting a price. The appraiser provides an objective opinion that's extremely valuable when making one of the most important financial decisions of your life.

Understand Cost Versus Value

In pricing your home, take time to understand the difference between cost and value. Consider one case, in which a homeowner had added solid platinum faucets in the bathrooms that cost $15,000. Such a purchase would never add $15,000 worth of value to the house—unless a buyer who feels passionate about platinum faucets steps forward (rather unlikely). The seller protested, "I just put in these new beautiful platinum faucets so it has to sell for a lot more." Not so.

Here is the defining question for the seller to answer: "If you had known you were going to sell your property in two months, would you have spent the money to install those $15,000 platinum faucets?"

"Probably not."

"Why?"

"Because I might not make that money back in the sale."

High-end sellers know that when they install something expensive in their properties—such as a home theater, a heated driveway, or a million-dollar sound system—they're unlikely to recover a commensurate amount when they sell. The typical buyer may not place the same value on these improvements and therefore may not be willing to pay you for them.

According to Jim Saben of Saben Appraisal Services on Cape Cod, Massachusetts, *cost* is what you pay; *value* is what you get. That means you mustn't expect all of the improvements made to the home to add value commensurate with their cost. Instead, look at the enjoyment you glean from having a pool or a finished basement as your personal return on investment.

Regression and Progression

The principle of regression says that when you build the most expensive house in the neighborhood, other properties will "pull down" the value of your house a little.

The principle of progression says when you have the smallest house in a neighborhood, the more expensive homes will "pull up" the value of your house a bit.

Do either of these principles apply to your particular situation? This is another reason why studying comparables in the area is so important.

Action Steps for Secret #3

Make a list of the special features in your home and ask the agents you interview if these features add value in your market.

Ask your agent(s) these questions:

What would the price of my home have to be, to sell it in 30 days?

What is your process for estimating sales price?

Secret #4: Luxury Home Sellers Understand the Time Value of Money

The luxury home sellers I have worked with know and understand that *a dollar today is worth more than a dollar tomorrow*. This maxim, referred to as the time value of money, is based on these four main reasons:

1. The sooner you invest, the higher the return. Obviously, if you invest a dollar today and it starts earning interest today, that dollar earns you more than the dollar you'd get a month, six months, or a year from now.

2. Inflation. In addition to interest-earning factors, inflation also makes a dollar worth more today, so tomorrow's dollar has less buying power. Even when the government reports the rate of inflation as relatively small, it still exists. And even if inflation is officially reported at only one or two percent, it sure feels higher to me when it comes to paying more for tuition, medical services, and filling my gas tank.

3. Ongoing Expenses. When talking about the dollar being worth more today than tomorrow in the context of real estate (or your house specifically), you must factor in ongoing expenses. Home ownership expenses include general maintenance, property taxes, repairs, and insurance coverage. In a level or declining market, if you can sell your house today and not have to pay for a month's worth (or two or three or six months' worth) of those expenses, you're ahead of the game.

When referring to the sale of your home, the only time a dollar today may not be worth more than a dollar tomorrow is in a fast-appreciating market. When your home's value increases quickly enough so the yearly change in value exceeds the costs of ownership, a dollar tomorrow can be worth more than a dollar today.

This maxim becomes even more powerful if you're selling to upgrade to a larger or newer home in an appreciating market. A more expensive home comes with higher ongoing expenses.

4. Unexpected Repairs. A dollar today is also worth more than a dollar tomorrow when you need to fund an unexpected repair. Say your water heater bursts, and your insurance doesn't cover its replacement or the resulting water damage. You're faced with the expense of removing the old water heater then buying and installing a new one: something you can't put off.

Such unexpected events that happen while your home is listed for sale confirms the maxim that every luxury seller knows—a dollar today is worth more than a dollar tomorrow, so take action today.

Use the Net Sheet

Many unsophisticated sellers tend to think in terms of absolute dollars rather than time-adjusted dollars. Their logic goes like this: "I want $400,000 for my house. And even if I have to wait two years to get that price, it's better than selling it today for $375,000." But is it?

The concept of time-adj Sheet illustration (Figure 1). In this example, your house is listed for sale at $300,000. Let's say you sell it today. After you cover the immediate selling expenses with the broker's fee of $18,000 and other expenses (e.g., tax stamps and transfer stamps) of $1,500, the net amount becomes $280,500.usted dollar value is demonstrated by the Net

Figure 1

Projected Net Sheet

All information contained herein is an estimate. All Sellers should verify with financial and legal professionals.

	Input	Nov-10 Closing (0)	1	3	6	9	12
Additional Months on Market from Today							
Projected selling price at different dates: Percentage	6%	$303,000	$300,000	$290,000	$280,000	$300,000	$325,000
Marketing Fee: Percentage	6%	$18,000	$18,000	$17,400	$16,800	$18,000	$19,500
Other							
Tax Stamps: Factor per $1,000	$5.00	$1,500	$1,500	$1,450	$1,400	$1,500	$1,625
Subtotal		$280,500	$280,500	$271,150	$261,800	$280,500	$303,875
Fed Capital Gains Tax on basis	20%	$6,100	$6,100	$4,230	$2,360	$6,100	$10,775
State Capital Gains Tax on basis	5%	$1,525	$1,525	$1,058	$590	$1,525	$2,694
Property Taxes Taxes			$225	$675	$1,350	$2,025	$2,700
Investment Opportunity Cost			$1,375	$3,988	$7,700	$12,375	$17,875
Insurance Costs			$183	$550	$1,100	$1,650	$2,200
Deed Preparation	$1,000	$1,000	$1,000	$1,000	$1,000	$1,000	$1,000
Title V Inspection	$350	$350	$350	$350	$350	$350	$350
Other Expense: maintenance	$0	$0	$200	$600	$1,200	$1,800	$2,400
Other Expense: repairs	$0	$0	$100	$300	$600	$900	$1,200
Smoke Detector Inspection	$50	$50	$50	$50	$50	$50	$50
Net to Seller		$271,475	$269,392	$258,350	$245,500	$252,725	$262,631

Estimated Basis for listed property	$250,000	
Estimated Annual Taxes	$2,700	per month: $225.00
Estimated Annual Insurance (Condo fees)	$2,200	per month: $183.33
Estimated Investment Opportunity Cost (%)	6%	Source:

(Typically seller's mortgage rate or locally available 5 yr. CD rate).

Then you make further subtractions for capital gains, insurance costs, and inspections. That gives you a net amount of $271,475. Do you see that the smarter move is to sell your house today for $300,000—rather than wait, and accumulate more expenses?

In contrast, look at the last column on the right. This is the seller who wants to hold out for $325,000, thinking the higher price is better, even if it takes a full year to sell. But though the price is $25,000 higher, the resulting net to seller—$262,631—is in fact less than the example of the immediate sale at a lower price.

This spreadsheet makes it easy to see why this is true. In a year's time, costs such as the mortgage, insurance, and general maintenance accrue on a month-by-month basis. They add up to a larger total expense that must be deducted from the sale price, even though that price is higher.

In addition to the general maintenance costs, let's consider the Investment Opportunity Cost of six percent, as noted in Figure 1. What exactly does this refer to? Investment Opportunity Cost is what you could possibly earn from investing the money you gain from the sale of your property.

Let's say you sold your house today for $300,000. You would then calculate where and how you could invest that money to receive a rate of return. You could use the figure that corresponds with what you can earn in the marketplace. If own your home with no mortgage, and could invest the entire net $300,000 at the time of sale, you could invest in a money market account and (as of the 2010 writing of this book) earn around one percent.

Most people, however, have a mortgage on their house. (I have always believed that the best investment anyone can make—one that earns a guaranteed return you can't match anywhere—is paying off your mortgage.)

The Net Sheet example shows an Investment Opportunity Cost of six percent, based on lost interest plus added costs, which is multiplied per month. As you can see, it begins with a monthly gain of $1,375, but after a full 12 months, you face the possibility of losing $17,875 in potential earnings.

To create calculations for your particular situation, go to www.JackCotton.com and download your own copy of the Net Sheet.

This online tool is extremely helpful to understand the concept of the time-value of money. It then becomes crystal clear that a dollar today in the sales price of your home is definitely worth more than a dollar down the road.

Change Your Mindset

Going back to the Net Sheet illustration in Figure 1, notice at the bottom line where it says "Net to Seller." You can see that if you sold your house today for $300,000, you would net $271,475. If you sell it even one month from now, your net will be about $1,000 less. The longer the property stays on the market, the more your net proceeds dwindle.

The luxury home seller would summarize the issue this way: "A dollar today is worth more than a dollar tomorrow." This is why I encourage sellers to change from thinking in terms of the absolute dollar to understanding the time-adjusted sales price of a property.

Ongoing expenses are not the only negative in having a house on the market for an extended period. The longer the sales time, the more aggravation you and your entire family experience. Dirty clothes must be picked up, beds made, dishes put away, and so on. You're constantly on call to have your place in a "show-ready" state.

In addition, the longer the property stays on the market, the more "shop-worn" it becomes and the more people will question why it's taking so long to sell. "Perhaps there's something wrong with it," they'll think. Potential buyers are more attracted to a home when others are, too, so they shy away from ones they think competing buyers don't want.

While the seller holds out for a higher price, the buyer who sees that the house has been on the market for six months or more is holding out for a big discount.

Check Your Ego

Strange as this may seem, I have talked to homeowners who, even after I explain this principle, simply don't care. Their egos dictate that they must chase the absolute dollar. They would rather receive $325,000 a year from now even if they net a lesser amount—just so they can tell people they got that $325,000.

Luxury home sellers know better.

The slower the real estate market, the more important this principle becomes. Declining market prices multiply the negative effect of carrying costs on the price of the home. As stated earlier, the only time this principle might not hold true would be during a real estate bubble when home prices increase at a rate that's greater than the total expenses to run the home plus opportunity costs. Only during these times would it *not* be detrimental to remain in the market a long time.

However, prices would have to be increasing at a significantly higher rate than the opportunity costs, for that reality to exist. Check the math. If your mortgage is six percent a year, plus all of your expenses, you have to hope that your property appreciates at nine to 12 percent a year for it to make sense to leave your house on the market for a long time. While that can happen—and it has happened in the past—the occurrence is rare.

What You Do with the Money

The next point, which the majority of sellers rarely consider, is what to do with the money once you sell your house.

Most luxury home sellers are clear about this. To them, the price they get matters less than what they do with the funds that result from the sale.

For example, in a soft market with a large supply of housing, buyers have a chance of finding an exceptional buy on a house. In that case, it's better to sell quickly and use that money to get back into the market quickly. You'd be wise to grab a stellar deal on another property that has suffered from drastic marketplace erosion. This way, what you gave up on the sale of your home will be more than made up in the purchase of your next one. I summarize the scenario like this: "What you can sell for, today, doesn't matter as much as what you can buy for, tomorrow." This is especially true in a buyer's market.

What happens if you sell your house to buy a larger one, in a market where prices are increasing?

Typically, when people move up, they tend to invest 50 percent more on their subsequent property than they did in their current one. That means if you were selling your house for $300,000, your next purchase would be around $450,000. If the market keeps going up, the gap will continue to widen with each passing day.

Realize that because the the house you're looking to purchase is at a higher price point, it's appreciating at a greater rate than the one you're selling. Therefore, you're wise to make the transaction sooner rather than later.

Don't Miss the Boat

Think of the market as a ship that's leaving the dock. The gap between the ship and the dock is steadily widening. The longer you wait to get the money from the sale of your house so you can invest in your next home, the wider the gap and the bigger the jump.

To realize the best values, aim to get the highest price that the current real estate market can support for your property, and execute that move as quickly as is feasible. That allows you to invest your money, get rid of your mortgage, stop the monthly expenses on this particular property, and start on the next phase of life.

Achieving Your Goals

You've set a goal for selling your property—one that can be realized sooner and more efficiently if you sell your property at the highest appropriate price the market can support.

If you think you can put a high price on your house and solve all your financial problems with that sale, it won't happen. Remember, buyers don't want to solve your financial problems by overpaying for your home.

Action Steps for Secret #4

Download the Net Sheet from my website at www.JackCotton.com

Experiment with different time and price scenarios to formulate your pricing strategy.

Secret #5: Luxury Home Sellers Know They Have to "Sell" Their Home Three Times

Most home sellers quickly become familiar with the home-selling routine when potential buyers come to look at their houses. They make the beds, clean the dishes, vacuum the floor, keep the pets' water and food dishes neat and the litter box empty. Sometimes this routine goes on for months on end. When they finally have an offer in hand, they breathe a huge sigh of relief, thinking, "I'm finally done with this. Now I can relax and just be myself until it's time to attend the closing and move everything out of here."

Not so fast.

Luxury home sellers know better. They understand that their house must be "sold" *two more times* before the deal fully closes. Enter the appraiser and the inspector.

Work with an Appraiser and "The Facts"

Of these two individuals, the appraiser is probably your home's harshest critic. This professional looks at everything in your house with zero emotion, like Joe Friday on the old TV show *Dragnet*, who always said, "Just the facts, ma'am."

The appraiser won't care about the happy memories you've accumulated in that home—the time your daughter came down that staircase to get married or all the great family get-togethers in the dining room and the backyard.

No. The appraiser looks at the cold, hard facts of the market— including nearby foreclosures. He or she will harshly assess the market value of your house and validate the price your buyer agreed to—or the sale may not go through. This is especially true since most buyers apply for a mortgage, subjecting the sale to a lender's scrutiny.

Use This Appraisal Checklist

Because this is such an important step in the sale of your home, you'll benefit from using this appraisal checklist to make sure everything gets covered in the process.

Before the buyer's appraiser arrives at your doorstep, ask about his or her license and certifications. You can also request a résumé to review his or her experience.

Not every appraisal assignment requires a licensed appraiser and not every appraiser is licensed. However, two instances require use of a licensed appraiser: (1) for a mortgage on home purchase and/or (2) for a refinance of your current mortgage. Remember, an appraiser looks at your home through the eyes of a typical buyer. (Exception: Even an appraiser can't predict the home's value to that once-in-a-lifetime buyer who wants to buy it because it joins his or her property, for example.)

Find out if the appraiser is familiar with the area. When followed carefully, appraisal standards result in an accurate value opinion no matter how much or how little local knowledge the appraiser has. However, reality can differ from theory. The appraiser's knowledge of the area can be your friend at valuation time.

Understand the difference between an appraisal and an agent's price opinion, known in the industry as a Competitive Market Analysis or CMA. The CMA presents one approach to estimating value by using comparable sales while the appraisal uses three approaches. In a professional appraisal, comparable sales are actually adjusted to compensate for differences between them and the subject property. The resulting appraisal documents are meant to support the value conclusion in an organized, systematic way.

Understand that the *appraised* value and the *assessed* value—the value assigned to your home by taxing authorities—are not necessarily the same. Assessed value is a value *assigned* to your property as of a certain date. That date can be 18 months in the past, which may not be close enough to the date you need your valuation for a refinance or purchase. Also, tax assessors cannot go out and visit thousands of properties each assessment period. Assessed valuations often rely heavily on computer models and not painstaking personal inspections of the property.

Don't be afraid to ask questions. Why were certain comparable sales chosen over others? How were the adjustments arrived at? A good appraiser will happily explain the calculations and value conclusions.

Make sure you or your agent has documents ready to simplify the appraiser's job. Topping the list of items you should have are: deed, plan, listing sheet, the agent's CMA, and the purchase agreement. Going the extra mile would include an assessor's field card, a septic location plan (if your home is not on a municipal sewer system), and listings of comparable properties.

Make a list of recent improvements or repairs to your home and give it to the appraiser when he or she arrives. Include newly installed roofs, septic system, heating and air-conditioning systems, etc. Even though cost and value are not the same, it can't hurt to provide this information.

Work with the Home Inspector

In addition to the appraiser, you must "sell" your house to the buyer's inspector. Why? Because the inspector's job is to assure the new buyer that no major undisclosed issues lurk beneath the surface in this house.

At the same time, for home inspectors to prove their worth to their clients, they have to find things wrong. If they don't, they're not perceived as doing their job well. Rarely does a home inspector go to a property, even a brand new one, and never find problems.

There's nothing wrong with selling a house that has issues; there's nothing wrong with selling a house that needs repairs; there's nothing wrong with buying a house that has defects. What *is* wrong is buying a property when these haven't been revealed at the outset. When the buyer becomes aware of these problems, the price gets negotiated to compensate for them. Assuming all of the areas of the property meet the buyer's needs, the transaction can then go forward.

So what is the best way to sell your house to an inspector, making sure that everything in the house is as it should be?

The easiest way requires a small investment many luxury home sellers willingly make: hiring a home inspector to look at the property before it goes on the market. This is called a pre-inspection. And if the inspector finds issues likely to trigger a negative response by the buyer's home inspector, the seller can deal with it by making necessary corrections or repairs before the eventual buyer even walks through the door.

Consider a Pre-Inspection

Having a pre-inspection by a licensed, qualified home inspector doesn't cost a lot. Most inspections run in the hundreds, not thousands, of dollars.

Most luxury home sellers know that either the buyer or the inspector will find something wrong; it's just a matter of time until they do. So if you're aware of an issue with your home and you believe no one will find out about it, you're sadly mistaken. People find out—always—and it's better to know sooner than later. In fact, it will cost you less if they find out sooner.

Luxury Home Sellers Know that Buyers Judge What They *Can't* See by What They *Can* See

In any house, you can't see the plumbing and wiring behind the walls; you can't see rot that might be taking place in the framing materials. But people do make assumptions, based on what they *can* see. So when there's rot under the door, shutters with peeling paint are hanging loose, or signs of water damage are visible on the ceilings or walls, judgments are made. When people do their own electrical work and the inspector sees uncovered electrical boxes or hanging wires in the basement, that creates a negative impression.

You remember that Secret #2 emphasized the importance of using experts. When it comes to selling your home, among those experts is an experienced real estate agent who knows the common home inspection pitfalls.

For instance, an agent walking up the front steps may see cracks in the joints between the bricks that allow the water to come through; the squishy board under the door that's rotten; loose or hanging gutters; plant life growing out of those gutters, and so on. A qualified real estate agent points out these things when initially examining your house. That agent will spot the potential problems and encourage you to get those items remedied before it's time for the buyer's inspector to show up. (This will be discussed further in Secret #7, staging and preparing the house.)

Look For These Items

There was a time in New England when people put asbestos shingles on their roofs, believing the asbestos would prevent a fire when sparks floated out of the chimney. Today, asbestos is considered a hazardous material and an involved process is required for removing and disposing of asbestos shingles.

Another common concern in the northeastern United States is underground oil tanks. Think back to the early 1970s when the nation suffered from the interruption in oil supply from the Middle East and you could only purchase gasoline on odd or even days. Many owners of luxury homes put 2,000-gallon oil tanks in the ground so they'd only need to buy heating oil once a year. But today, like asbestos shingles, those tanks have to be removed. I guarantee you it's cheaper to remedy these situations before a buyer comes along than after. Don't hesitate to hire a qualified, licensed person to address these issues on your property.

Here's a problem I often see. Owners of a heavy piece of furniture like a piano or a chest or armoire will purchase an adjustable Lally column to deal with the object's excessive weight. They set up the Lally column in the basement, in the middle of that area holding up the heavy piece, and tighten it until the floor doesn't squeak anymore. I can assure you that portable Lally columns in a basement will trigger a skeptical eye from a home inspector. It's a clear sign of a potential structural problem. You're best to figure out how to rectify that situation so that a column won't be present when your house is being inspected. By this, I don't mean simply remove the portable column. I mean talk to a qualified builder about fixing the problem properly.

Leaks in the ceilings or walls need to be addressed. Seal them and paint over the stains—but, more important, locate the source of the leak and make sure you fix it properly. It shows a lack of integrity to patch over the symptoms and not pinpoint the cause.

View Your Home Through Cold, Heartless Eyes

Realize that, as a homeowner, you see your home every day through the eyes of your heart. But when the potential buyer, the appraiser, and the inspector come through, they see your house through the cold, calculating heartless eyes that their role in the transaction requires. A luxury home seller has no trouble understanding that fact.

As noted earlier, you can prepare for the home inspector by getting a pre-inspection before your home goes on the market. At the very least, hire an agent who has experience selling homes like yours in your area. That agent will be familiar with the common problems home inspectors are finding in your neighborhood. That way, you can deal with those items before the home goes on the market.

It's a fact that buyers tend to *horribilize* (a word from my friend and real estate speaker Howard Brinton) anything they see wrong with the house. If they notice a problem, they magnify it. Why? When a house needs a dollar's worth of work, a sharp buyer will try to knock three to five dollars off the price. That's why luxury home sellers make sure their homes are show-ready and perfect. And they understand they have to sell it three times to prevent that erosion in value when the sale occurs.

Action Steps for Secret #5

Make sure your agent has a package of materials ready for the appraiser.

Ask if your agent intends to be present during the appraisal and inspection visits.

Pay special attention to the details in Secret 7.

Walk around your home and see it with cold, heartless eyes.

List every item you see that could present a problem to a prospective buyer's inspector.

Make a plan to deal with any repairs *now* so a buyer will have no reason to *horribilize* your property and negotiate a lower price.

Secret #6: Luxury Home Sellers Know What to Expect From Marketing

An important factor in selling a home is understanding both the purpose of marketing, and what to expect from it.

My friend, speaker, and gifted real estate agent Walter Sanford refers to the Real Estate God (REG) in his talks. He says REG is at work when an agent, most often coerced by an anxious seller, buys an expensive ad in a glossy magazine. A buyer then responds to that ad and—amazingly—immediately pays full price for the house. REG stories, often repeated by advertising salespeople, result in lots of money being spent—and often wasted—in lottery-like marketing.

REG: It's Like Winning the Lottery

Depending on REG to sell your house bears a lot of similarity to buying a winning lottery ticket. Remember: Winning doesn't happen regularly, it's never something you can rely on, and it's not an action you can readily duplicate.

Nevertheless, as the REG story gets out, sellers hear about it and demand the same expensive full-page ad when their own houses go on the market. They believe in quantity—that is, the more ads that feature their house, the more likely the property will sell fast. After all, a REG story (and not necessarily a recent one) validates their position.

Find Out What's Going On Behind the Scenes

Seeing their properties' ads is usually the only visible evidence sellers have of the marketing work done on their behalf. And so the size of the ad, the number of pictures, and their frequency of use are factored in. Other than potential buyers actually viewing the home, ads are often the only barometer of activity that's being done on their behalf.

But if you have a sharp agent, you can expect serious work to be going on behind the scenes. You may have no way of knowing that the agent is making countless phone calls every day to people who might buy this particular house. The seller has no knowledge of (or rarely gets to see) mailings that go to hundreds of potential buyers who could be interested in this house. Because sellers can't see this aspect, they mostly focus on the advertising. Therefore, it has become customary for sellers to put a lot of credence in advertising.

Often, sellers select their agents on the basis of who has the most ads posted. Why? Because they think that more ads will mean a quicker, higher sale price. Mostly, it's because they don't understand the process.

On the other hand, those in the real estate business know that advertising tends to be the most expensive and least effective way to find a buyer for a property. Rarely does it lead to a sale with the highest price, in the shortest time, with the least amount of aggravation.

Avoid the Ineffective Five-P Plan

Because sellers in the high-end market understand this, they demand to see their agent's complete marketing plan. And it had better not be the Five-P Plan that's most common in today's real estate industry.

The Five-P Plan is a minimal one:

1. Put the house in MLS (Multiple Listing Service)
2. Put a sign in the yard.
3. Put an ad in the paper.
4. Pat the seller on the back.
5. Pray it will sell.

This is *not* the marketing plan you should rely on.

Yes, when properly used, advertising can create a sense of urgency and it can create traffic. Ads placed locally may be seen by someone in that area who wants to buy something that's bigger or better located than their current home. Reading the ad, they've now become aware of your property. Plus, seeing the ad gives them a greater sense of urgency. They think, "Because other people will see this ad, I'd better move on it quickly and aggressively."

In some cases, then, ads can be used to create traffic. However, the luxury home seller and most agents know that those who actually look at print real estate ads are other sellers assessing the competition and deciding which real estate company has the most or biggest ads.

Buyers Use Ads to Eliminate Options

When buyers respond to ads, they're typically calling to eliminate possibilities. Think of the last time you bought something from a classified ad. You sat down with a cup of coffee, a newspaper, and a pen. You opened it to the classified section, then began circling a bunch of ads offering something that interested you: a car, a boat, gardening equipment—whatever.

Next, you began the process of eliminating possibilities. You made phone calls with the goal of drawing lines through those ads you circled to eliminate them as quickly as possible.

The scene is no different when someone is buying a house. Imagine that your little ad gets placed right next to a big one written by a qualified, trained, professional agent with a staff of people who know how to create compelling real estate ads. You run the chance of having the ad for your house eliminated quickly. That's why it's not the most effective way to market your home.

The whole idea of advertising is to create a sense of competition among prospects who are either directly interested in your house or have friends or associates who might be interested.

People often think that when their house goes on the market, they need to find a buyer from far away— preferably from overseas. In my experience, buyers typically come from just around the corner. They could be relocating from another city, but they could be someone right in your neighborhood or, at the very least, a friend of someone in the area. Marketing, when done correctly, can create that sense of urgency from a buyer already in your town. Why? Because local buyers think that the far-away buyer may call on the house and compete with them to acquire it.

Luxury home sellers know that marketing or advertising won't sell a house all by itself. If your house is overpriced for the market, you could spend millions of dollars for a 30-second Super Bowl ad—and still not sell it.

Indeed, if ads alone sold real estate consistently, there would be no real estate agents or companies.

Create a Marketing Plan With a Mix

Luxury home sellers know that for successful agents to get the right price for their properties, they need a marketing plan that has a mix of everything: Direct mail campaigns, print campaigns, Internet strategy, open houses to other agents and consumers, and most important, the agent's sphere of influence and customer base.

This is why it's hard for home sellers to sell a house by themselves as a "For Sale By Owner" (FSBO). The following story makes this point clear.

Let's say you walked into a clothing store to purchase a new suit but found only one suit available. It's blue—not your color—and it's not your size. What can you do? Because the shop owner doesn't have what you want, you walk out. You're specifically looking for a store with lots of inventory from which you can choose the style, color and size you want.

I once had a commercial tenant who owned a ladies' clothing store. She has passed away, but in her day, she was one of the smartest business people I've ever known. I often heard her quote her uncle, who told her,

"Darlene, you can't sell from an empty cart. Even if you're selling stuff like crazy out of your store, always make sure you have a lot of inventory, because that's what brings people in."

Let's apply that principle to selling your home by yourself. You put an ad in the paper, people circle it, and then they call. It's extremely easy for them to draw a line through your ad and go on to the next one. You've only got that one house for sale.

A real estate agent who has a lot of listings, though, offers a full inventory. When a potential buyer calls on the ad, that agent is trained to know the right questions to ask. (Visit www.JackCotton.com for a list of the questions.) Seldom does a buyer call up and purchase the exact house they saw in the ad. The agent asks probing questions and suggests other properties that might interest them. (And yours might be among them.)

The final truth that luxury home sellers know about advertising is that buyers tend to "buy up" on ads and "buy down" on signs.

Real estate ads usually sound fantastic, making even the dullest property sound like a palace. But what often happens? A potential buyer will read an ad and think, "Here's a home that sounds perfect and it's only $500,000. We'd expected to have to pay $700,000 to get all this."

Potential buyers call on the ad, and when they view the property in person, most rule it out and buy a home that is, on average, 50 percent more expensive than the one advertised—one that sells for $750,000 in this example.

Conversely, people tend to "buy down" on signs. When my wife and I were looking for a second home in Naples, Fla., we passed a quintessential "old Florida" cottage—stucco, with off-kilter shutters and overgrown landscaping—near the water, with a For Sale sign out front. It looked like our perfect fantasy of a Florida getaway home.

When we called the listing agent, we learned that the asking price was more than $20 million. Just a bit out of our range. We did ultimately buy a home—but way, way down on the price scale.

This happens with many buyers. They drive by a property with a For Sale sign out front and wonder, *"How expensive can this place be?"* only to find out it costs five times more than they'd planned to invest.

Doctors Diagnose and Prescribe

Let's look at another analogy. When you're in the FSBO category and someone calls, you're like a doctor with only aspirin to prescribe. If the patient calls up with a stomach ailment and all you have is aspirin, you're not going to be very helpful. On the other hand, the doctor who has a large inventory of medicines can not only diagnose the problem, but provide the right medication.

In the same way, the real estate agent with a full cart of listings can diagnose the wants, needs, and desires of the caller and then prescribe the property that meets those criteria. With such an agent on your team, you've just increased your chances that your house will meet someone's needs.

Here's yet another situation in which agents can be beneficial. There may have been a home advertised six months ago that caused a potential buyer to call an agent. That home may no longer be available, but your home comes on the market and it's the perfect one for that buyer.

I'm not trying to say that all advertising is a waste of time or money. Advertising has its place, but it's both expensive and passive. You buy an ad and wait for something to happen.

In contrast, when you hire a great agent, you can expect active marketing: calling prospective buyers, reaching out to neighbors, calling other agents, and using the database of the agent or company.

So when you're selling your home, it makes a huge difference to be working with an agent or company that has a full cart of options, not an empty one, and knows how to qualify callers using key questions.

Adopt realistic goals about marketing and understand the purpose of advertising. Be aware of what it can accomplish and what it cannot. Only then will your expectations be met.

Action Steps for Secret #6

Make a list of all the times you have purchased anything from a classified ad.

How many items did you circle?

How many sellers did you call?

Did you finally buy the item advertised?

Review your agent interview questions from Secret #2, working with experts, to make sure you are clear on your marketing expectations.

Secret #7: Luxury Home Sellers Know the Value of Preparing Their Property for Sale

Some refer to this as "staging," but it's so much more than that. In a soft market, with many homes for sale, the exceptional home will sell faster than the rest. The exceptional home will be the one that's ready to be moved into, the one in pristine condition. With no work required, the family can pack up and move in as soon as the deal closes. The homes that need work—with lots of deferred maintenance—will take longer to sell.

Do You Cut In at the Checkout Line?

Compare selling your home to waiting in a long checkout line at the supermarket. The only difference is, when you're in the "house for sale" checkout line, you wait your turn for the cashier to give you the money for your house

You know what it's like to stand in a long line of shoppers at the supermarket checkout where only one cashier patiently checks everyone out. Now imagine the uproar if someone were to cut in, move up, and check out sooner than the rest.

Selling your home is like waiting in the real estate checkout line with 20 carts (or 20 homes) waiting in turn to get to the cashier (the buyer) to be paid for the house. But in this scenario, you're allowed to cut in line *and* you don't upset others by doing it.

List at Right Price and Keep It Show-Ready

You accomplish that in two ways: You list your home at the right price and make sure it's in the best condition of those on the market.

Overpriced homes that need work will keep moving farther back in the line. They can see the checkout and the cashier, but they never quite get there because other sellers keep cutting in line and moving ahead of them.

Luxury home sellers keep their houses show-ready even when they have no intention of selling them soon. They have a routine, a schedule, and a plan for maintaining their properties.

You can emulate this practice, while being economical, by doing constant maintenance, like painting one side of your house every year. Do the front this year, the east side next year, the south side the year after that, and so on. That way, nothing falls to rack and ruin.

Maintain Up-To-Date Photos

It's also wise to have current photos of your home on hand at all times. You never know when your plans might change or when the mood might strike to just sell your house and buy another. That's why it's practical to maintain a file of seasonal photos for your property. If you live in a resort area, as I do in Cape Cod, and you put your house on the market in the winter, current exterior photos will look dismal. They won't attract anyone.

Likewise, if you reside in Lake Tahoe, California, or Sun Valley, Idaho, prospective buyers will want to see your house buried in snow. So always maintain an up-to-date file of seasonal photos. That way, if you put your house on the market in the off-season, you have great photos to make your house stand out from all the others.

It's my practice to photograph every waterfront house in my market at least every other summer. That way, when sellers call to list their houses in the winter, I have seasonal photos on hand. When the bay freezes and ice washes up on the beaches, I can show beautiful summer shots of all of the properties. It makes a huge difference.

You can do the same for your property.

Develop a Staging Checklist

Luxury home sellers use a staging checklist to maximize curb appeal and get their homes show-ready. As Will Rogers said, "You never get a second chance to make a first impression."

When you place your house on the market, the first impression counts for everything. If weeds are taking over the lawn and shutters are peeling, that's not a good first impression. Remember that potential buyers judge what they *can't* see by what they *can* see. If they see negative things before they even step out of the car in front of your house, their imaginations go wild. A negative initial impression never bodes well for the rest of their experience as they tour your property.

Check the landscaping. Pull the weeds and look for overgrown tree limbs that touch the house. Paint the trim, or at least your front door and entryway. If you have pets, clean up their outdoor play area. A potential buyer cannot appreciate the wonders of your home if they have to watch every step they make in your yard.

Seeing your own home through your heart, not your eyes, also applies to your sense of smell. When you go through your house, your "nose" gets turned off because you love your dog or kitty. But animal smells may jolt a stranger who walks into your house for the first time. Don't leave a negative first impression; clean the floors and carpets thoroughly—and keep them that way.

Also be careful what you cook when your house is on the market. If you like to host an exotic food festival or a chili cook-off, find a better time to do it in case it creates lingering smells.

If you have a basement, be sure to check it, too. Is it clean and well organized? I typically encourage sellers to vacuum the tops of all their pipes. That way, when someone goes down to the basement and sees clean, dust-free pipes and a furnace and boiler that looks new, that buyer assumes everything that can't be seen is also shipshape. It's a subconscious conclusion.

I often say to a seller, "If you paint anything, paint the basement. Paint the walls white, paint the floors light gray, and make it sparkle." Then a potential buyer will think, "Boy, if it's really in super shape down here, the rest of the house must be in great condition."

Selling your house means packing and moving, so I suggest people begin that process early. Pack things you use infrequently that normally lie out on the kitchen and bathroom counters. Clean out your closets to make them look bigger. Purchase attractive baskets and put stray items in them.

Plant flowers outside and place green plants and bouquets on the inside. Make sure windows are clean, not so grimy and dirty that sunlight can't get through them.

Also, add extra-high-wattage light bulbs among your lights. If you have 60-watt bulbs, especially in some of the dark rooms, replace them with 75- to 100-watt bulbs (as long as your lamps are rated to accept that extra wattage). Any house looks much better when it's lit up and bright.

Consider calling a staging expert, someone who specializes in staging homes for sale. However, if you choose the right real estate agent, he or she can offer great ideas about what's required to get your home ready for the market. Professional agents use checklists to help you accomplish that. In our agency, we have a 10-page checklist that goes room by room to ensure that everything will show perfectly. It includes such items as installing a new gasket on the dishwasher, vacuuming the pipes in the basement, eliminating all water stains, and getting rid of clutter.

Cutting clutter means putting away most family photos. If people see too many family photos around, they can't imagine themselves living in your house. They'll feel like interlopers, and they won't be able to see past all those photos.

That said, you want to leave out a few photos because it makes dealing with you seem more personal. Again, a staging expert or sharp agent can help you with any details you might not be aware of.

Make a Show-Day Checklist

Be sure to follow a separate checklist on days an agent shows your property to prospective buyers. Items that enhance a showing include playing soft music in the background (I recommend classical music). Turn on lights and open window treatments so light can shine in and outside views are visible. Make sure beds are made, toilet seats are down, random objects are picked up and put away. For the most part, use your common sense. And take your time. Prepare your house slowly. If you're in a hurry you might forget something.

Imagine that you're a pilot going through a checklist before takeoff. For example, the islands of Martha's Vineyard and Nantucket are located not far off Cape Cod. Nantucket is only 26 miles away, but because it's a long boat ride, most people take a 10-minute flight. In fact, the pilot flies to Nantucket multiple times a day. You might be surprised to know that even on those little planes, the pilot pulls out a checklist before even firing up the engine. Going through the checklist guarantees that nothing gets overlooked or forgotten; the pilot takes nothing for granted even on a 10-minute flight.

Similarly, you should take nothing for granted on what may be only a 10-minute showing.

Many times, a last-minute phone call limits your time to get your home prepared for a showing. Having your checklist helps ensure you don't forget something important. Run through your list quickly—just like the pilot does, *every time* before heading down the runway—to maximize the sales value of your home. It's exactly what a luxury home seller would do.

What Happens When a House Stands Empty?

Sometimes a seller has already moved and the house stands empty. In this case, your strategy would be different. Do you stage the home by bringing in furniture and decorative appointments? There's no set answer for this because it varies from house to house. Sometimes I recommend the seller not take everything out. For instance, in a home that has a combination living/dining room, you definitely need furniture in that area so buyers won't have to imagine how the single space can work as two separate living areas.

I've known sellers who make arrangements with a local decorator or furniture store owner to lend pieces of furniture. In addition to supplying the furniture, they're allowed to put placards on the pieces saying "Furnishings courtesy of ABC Furniture Company." The furniture store owner anticipates the buyers will want to buy what's in place, and sometimes they do. But even if they don't, at least the store gets publicity it otherwise wouldn't enjoy.

If there are no furnishings, buyers who don't have great imaginations might walk in and say, "Gosh, how can we fit our dining table and the whole living room set in this space? I don't see how that can be done." When the space displays the furniture already set up, it's easier to visualize. If your home has all separate rooms, then it's not as critical.

Another important room to stage is the master bedroom. Real estate agents often hear people say, "I don't see how you can fit a king-size bed in this room and still be able to open the drawers in the dresser." You have to show the prospective buyer that it can be done.

Some believe that trying to sell an empty house is the kiss of death. I don't agree. In fact, sometimes a sale comes more easily when the house *isn't* filled with furniture. One major advantage to keeping the house empty is that it can be shown at a moment's notice.

Suppose your agent is out with buyers who express interest in a colonial style house and your house is a ranch style. Although your home might not top the list to show that buyer, the more the agent talks and gets to know the people, the more the agent thinks, "I know he wants a colonial, but he also wants a beautiful backyard with specimen tree plantings and a place located close to the town center, so I'll show them this ranch style." They drive over and tour it immediately. And—*voilà*—

they end up buying your house. That can't always happen when your home remains occupied.

Also with an empty house, all visual distractions are gone. Potential buyers can envision it with their own furniture and belongings in place.

Of course, an empty home must be clean. No cobwebs in the corners; no bugs or critters homesteading. If you can't take care of details like this regularly, hire someone who can, or the house will appear neglected and shopworn. It won't seem as enticing to potential buyers, and its value will begin to dwindle. Even if your house stands empty, you can make sure it smells like lemon oil or another fresh fragrance. That's a sign someone's caring for the property. Even such small details will create a positive aura for potential buyers.

Action Steps for Secret #7

1. Create a staging checklist for your home.
2. Visit www.StagedHomes.com for tips.
3. Go through your home with the checklist and start making a list of what needs to be completed before you put your house on the market.

Secret #8: Luxury Home Sellers Avoid Common Mistakes When Selling Their Homes

To sell your house as a luxury home seller would, pay attention to seven common mistakes and learn to avoid them. You want to:

1. **Avoid hiring a real estate agent because of a high listing price recommendation.**

Some real estate agents might suggest a high listing price for your home, hoping to entice you to sign a contract to work together. Indeed, doing this is an actual business model for certain real estate practitioners who want to control the inventory in a given market. They inflate their price opinions to get listings, making each home a "billboard" to promote their brokerage business. They don't really care if your home sells—so long as a reasonable percentage of their listings sell, so that they can stay in business.

This practice prevails mostly with companies or agents trying to break into a new market. Controlling the listing inventory allows them to create a "pipeline" of listing transactions. A home comes on the market at an inflated price—and then the brokers will slowly reduce the price over the term of the contract. If they can keep the contract on the listed property for the year or so it takes to sell, they finally get paid.

With any agent, make sure you receive a recommendation for pricing your home *in writing*—as well as comparable sales and competing offerings. Ask how the agent arrived at the price. As flattering as it may be to hear a larger-than-anticipated number for your home, seek the truth. What's the true market value?

Also ask the agent to drive you by the comparable sales, and homes similar to yours currently on the market. Remember, the market sets the ultimate price for your home, not the agent. Your agent's job is to get you the highest price possible *that can be supported by the market.*

2. Avoid hiring an agent for reasons other than their qualifications.

Let's face it, with so many people holding real estate licenses today, it's likely you have a friend or relative selling real estate in your area.

Now, would you hire a heart surgeon based on friendship, or would you base your choice on the surgeon's skill, experience, and record of accomplishment? Next to a medical emergency, few decisions are more important than those dealing with the purchase or sale of your home, so work with the right expert. Ask for the agent's résumé, track record, and written marketing plan. Does he or she guarantee the work in writing? Remember, selling your home calls for putting *your* interests first.

3. Avoid excluding potential buyers from your listing contract.

It's not uncommon for neighbors, friends, or visitors to express interest in purchasing your property should you decide to sell. It's tempting to think you can sell your home to one of them and save the cost of an agent's commission or marketing fee. Guess what? Buyers think the same way, and will subtract their high estimate of a real estate fee from their offer. It's important to determine your agent's negotiating skills and qualifications. An experienced negotiator almost always realizes a price that covers the sales fee and then some. This is partly because a neutral third party is in a better position to negotiate than the buyers and sellers themselves (especially when you have a personal relationship). Also, the buyers feel pressure when your agent actively markets your property at the time they express interest. The bottom line: The buyer wants the house price to be discounted by the amount of the marketing fee, while the seller hopes to not have to pay it. Both the buyer and the seller *cannot* save the same fee.

4. Avoid restricting access to your home.

Unquestionably, living in a home that's for sale can be aggravating. However, this fact remains true: The easier it is to show your home, the more it will get shown. The more it gets shown, the more likely you are to receive an offer, which shortens the entire marketing process. I recommend lock boxes, but at the very least, make sure your agent has access to a key and can show your home anytime (after giving you notice, of course). Let your agent know it's okay to come and show it if you don't answer the phone.

I love it when a seller says, "We only want our home shown on the second and fourth Saturdays of the month, after two in the afternoon when there is a north wind and clear skies and the planets aren't in retrograde." I exaggerate here, but any real estate agent can give you examples of sellers restricting access that are almost that extreme—and not exaggerated at all.

5. Avoid falling into the selling-season trap.

Sellers often ask about the best time of year to sell a home: spring, summer, winter, or fall. The answer is simple. Put your home on the market when the time is right for *you.*The market is busy all year long, and the only market you can be certain of is today's. Waiting for a better selling season won't give you much advantage if interest rates suddenly rise or if the stock market corrects, for instance. The best timing is when *you* feel ready.

6. Avoid over-testing the market.

By pricing your home too high or not being committed to your decision to sell, you run the risk of putting a stigma on your property. Overpriced homes tend to stay on the market for a long period and become shopworn, as noted earlier.

In addition, if you're not sure whether you want to sell and you turn down a valid offer or cancel a contract, you run the risk of raising questions about your property. People will ask, "What's wrong with it?"

7. Don't ignore recommendations on preparing your home for sale.

Remember, buyers tend to *horribilize* problems they see in a home. While no scientifically proven ratio exists, experience shows that for every $100 of work your home may require, buyers will expect a reduction of $300 to $500 from the sale price. In many cases, painting and minor repairs bring returns far exceeding their cost. So prepare your home for sale based on your agent's expert advice before the first showing. Remember, you never get a second chance to make a positive first impression.

Action Steps for Secret #8

Copy the list of common seller mistakes from this secret and keep it handy when your home goes on the market.

Talk to at least three friends or associates who sold a home in the past 12 months. Discuss these points:

What was the biggest mistake they made in selling their homes?

Name three things they would have done differently.

What were the three best things that occurred during the process of selling their homes?

Secret #9: Luxury Home Sellers Expect Feedback and Don't Take It Personally

When luxury home sellers put a house on the market, they want and expect feedback. They don't interpret that feedback as a personal attack *and* they don't shoot the messenger when they receive it. Because they're accustomed to working with large, high-end transactions, they've learned to distance themselves emotionally from what's happening in the transaction.

Ask for Feedback

Talk to your agent and find out what feedback you'll receive—that is, what kinds of reports you'll be given noting the activity that takes place.

We've noted previously that print advertising is, in most cases, the only evidence most sellers have that activity is happening in their behalf. It doesn't have to be that way. Ask what you can expect. Tell your agent you *want* to be informed about actions taken to get your home ready for sale or presented to a buyer.

Make It Easy for Other Agents

When your agent shows your house to other local agents—either from his or her company or from the Multiple Listing Service (MLS)—hearing the comments they make is critical in understanding how the market will perceive your offering. Remember, these professionals work in the market every day. Listen carefully to what they have to say, especially about price. Getting that feedback early in the process allows you to make adjustments sooner rather than later.

For instance, perhaps during the MLS tour, several agents say, "This is really a great house. We love the area and think the house is priced right but, man, you've got to do something about the litter box in the laundry room."

Your agent may have been reluctant to bring up the subject with you, the seller, but because other agents commented on it, it's not easy to ignore. So your agent might say to you, "During the MLS tour, three or four of our agents pointed out the same thing. It isn't something we noticed at first, but after listening to them, I feel I have to bring it up. Something needs to be done about the litter box in the laundry room."

Keep in mind that when other agents come through your home, bringing years of experience, their feedback is critical. Whatever they say, you need not—and must not—take it personally. No one thinks you're a bad person. Simply trust your agent enough to take the right action on the feedback. Your purposes are aligned; you want to get your home sold for the highest market price possible.

Getting activity through showings or over the Internet, but not getting offers, likely means something is "off" with your house. Usually it's the price, but other elements could be at play, too. Take feedback as a sign to make adjustments or repairs.

Listen to Mr. Market

Luxury home sellers know not to take feedback personally because, for the most part, they know Mr. Market is talking. Mr. Market can be cruel; he has zero emotion; he doesn't care about your house except how it fits into the marketplace. He's all about the numbers.

Understand that a good agent helps you set the best price that Mr. Market will *allow* at any given time. To get feedback from Mr. Market, ask your agent for these ratios:

1. What is the average list-to-sales price ratio in my market?
2. What is the average time for a house in my category and area to be on the market?
3. What is the average price per square foot of homes sold within my market?
4. What are the assessment ratios in my area? In other words, how do sales prices on houses in my neighborhood compare to those houses' tax assessments?

Together, this valuable information gives you an idea of what's going on.

Make Needed Adjustments

When information isn't in their favor, luxury home sellers know not to shoot the messenger. They don't replace one agent with another who'll say what they want to hear. Mr. Market's telling you to make adjustments, which might even mean taking your home off the market for a while.

Our family owns a small place in Florida that we bought shortly before the market peaked—about 10 minutes before the peak. We didn't get to use it as much as we thought we would, so we put it on the market for what we thought was a great price compared to the amount we'd put into it.

However, Mr. Market's feedback said people thought our property was worth 30 percent less than we did, and we were 20 percent below our cost. This represented a huge loss to us.

We had to adjust—either lower the price or take it off the market and wait for things to change. In our case, we took it off the market and we'll wait for market conditions to change before trying to sell it again. That could be five years down the road.

That was a case of Mr. Market speaking. Unless REG (the Real Estate God) shines down on your house, you might have to wait for the market to shift. That's how the laws of economics work.

Fortunately, our family didn't need to sell in a hurry. In some cases, though, people do have to sell immediately—and that can lead to their taking a loss or setting up a "short sale" in which they sell a house for less than they owe on the mortgage.

Years ago, when I owned my own company and had agents working for me, I'd come into a sales meeting wearing a giant baby pacifier on a ribbon around my neck. I'd say to the agents in the group, "To an agent, taking a listing with a price that's way off the mark is like a pacifier to a baby. It makes you feel good—'Hey, great; I got a listing!'—but you won't get anything from it. It won't sell. That pacifier makes you feel like you're a real estate pro, but you're not."

Of course, you can always choose not to listen to whatever the market says to do differently, but luxury home sellers know that putting a home on the market for the wrong price wastes everyone's time. Now you face a choice: Either you adjust to the market or decide not to participate in it at all.

Action Steps for Secret #9

Go to www.Zillow.com and enter the address of your property.

1. Count the number of homes that would compete with yours if it came on the market today.
2. Count the number of homes that sold in your area in the past 12 months.

Divide the two numbers to calculate the absorption rate. For example, say there are 30 homes for sale and 10 sold in the past 12 months. That means the absorption rate for homes like yours right now is three years. So with no change in the market, it would take three years for the current volume of inventory to be sold off.

There is no ideal absorbtion rate but a 3 month rate is better than a 3 year rate. The lower the number, the more aggressive you can be with your initial offering price. An absorbtion rate that is in years rather than months does not bode well for a high sales price.

Secret #10: Luxury Home Sellers Know a Picture's Worth a Million Words

When it comes to the adage "a picture's worth a thousand words," luxury home sellers change it to "a picture can be worth a *million* words."

When selling your house, you want more than one picture. You also want the right photos shot in the right way by the right person: an experienced pro who knows how to photograph high-end properties.

As discussed in Secret #6, in this day of advanced technology, people are turning away from print media and are marketing on the Internet because it's immediate and can be updated any time, day or night.

In a print ad for a home, you might see one black-and-white photo of that home, the size of a postage stamp. On the Internet, though, you can take a full tour of a house featuring dozens of photos that show all areas.

Don't Skimp on Photography

Don't spare the expense; hire the best real estate professional photographer in your area. Here's why:

Potential buyers will often eliminate your property from consideration immediately, based on poor photography. If you have to skimp on marketing your property, professional photography is not the place to do it.

You won't get results if you shoot photos with an ordinary point-and-shoot camera—yet people use such photos all the time. An inferior camera will give you pictures of dark rooms, with big blinding spots where the windows are. Not acceptable.

Jack Cotton

For the absolute best effects, hire someone who knows how to operate a sophisticated camera with a wide-angle lens and high resolution, and especially understands the dynamics of light.

A professional photographer (and sometimes a talented agent) can work a camera so you not only see a room's interior, but also the scene outside the window. That requires equalizing the interior and exterior light with a manually operated camera and usually one or more external flashes. You simply can't do that with your automated point-and-shoot camera.

Another process that allows for fantastic depiction of a room and the exterior views is High Dynamic Range (HDR) photography.

This method can eliminate the need for a high-powered flash to light up a large room. The photographer takes up to nine photos of the same shot, each at a different shutter speed. This is also referred to as bracketing. Many high-end cameras are programmed to take the nine shots automatically.

Once the photos are downloaded to a computer, the best elements of the nine photos will create one perfect shot for each scene. This method is a little labor-intensive and requires a professional but the results are stunning.

Be Selective in Your Choices

Once you've chosen a photographer, you want to be selective in what rooms get photographed. For instance, most buyers aren't interested in seeing photos of the bathrooms. Unless your master bathroom looks like a luxury spa with acres of marble, huge showers, and a giant Jacuzzi tub, you can skip bathroom photography completely.

Mostly, you're looking for photos that exude a desirable lifestyle. Begin with a great picture of the front of the house, then zoom in on the entryway. Take photos of rooms as if someone were living in them so viewers can imagine themselves enjoying the space.

Take time to set the dining table with proper place settings before the photo shoot. Light a fire in the fireplace. Clear off countertops. Use the staging checklist in Secret #7 to prepare for the photography session.

Remember, these photos make up a living, ongoing representation of your property. If the scenes are full of clutter or poorly lit so people can't tell what's in the rooms, that's inadequate representation and it certainly won't help you get your property displayed well and sold.

Take Photos at Optimum Times

It's usually impossible to photograph a whole house in one appointment because the sun lies in different positions in the sky at certain times of the day. For example, you don't want the sun shining at the camera when shooting the front of your house. So the photographer (your agent or a professional photographer) should look around the property and come up with a photo plan that answers the question, "At what time do I need to come here to photograph which side?" It might be necessary to shoot the front elevation in the morning and the back in the afternoon.

The photo plan includes knowing the best time of the day and season of the year for shooting quality photographs. In our Cape Cod market, we have a difficult time taking exterior photos in the autumn. As we get into the early fall months of September and October—no matter what time of day—we can never get a good shot of houses, especially if trees are present. The front exteriors of the homes always look dark because the sun is low and the shadows are long.

On the other hand, if your yard has no trees, wonderful shots are possible in autumn because the light is a golden hue and the sky a vivid blue. In your area, fall might be the best season for shooting. Be aware and act accordingly.

Action Steps for Secret #10

Find a good photographer in your area and arrange to have photos taken during your home's "prime time."

Alternatively, decide on the real estate agent you will work with to sell your home and have him or her arrange for the photos even if they'll be used at a later date.

Secret #11: Luxury Home Sellers Leave No Stones Unturned

Luxury home sellers know that, to get the highest price for their properties in the least amount of time with the smallest amount of aggravation, they must leave no stone unturned.

Put Together an Idea-Filled Plan

Every item covered in this book, even though it may seem minor, needs to go into a plan with its activities executed almost simultaneously. Why? Because you want your property to go on the market with a big splash—a sense of "shock and awe," or something close. That means you want it to create excitement, build enthusiasm, and generate a sense of urgency.

I've had home sellers say they want to put their house on the market but keep it out of the MLS for a month or so, just to see what happens. Other times, real estate agents will suggest exposing the offering of your home to their company client list for a period of time before listing in the local MLS. A luxury home seller, on the other hand, knows that you want to be like the landing of marines on a beachhead: you want to take the market by storm.

Don't just pick out one or two ideas trying to see which works. When selling your house, use all your ideas—and all at once. After the sale closes, once you have the buyer's check in hand—*then* you can relax. But there's no time to relax while your home is on the market.

You have the power to make sure that your house is the first one in the checkout line and you aren't getting pushed to the back. Don't waste time making changes in price or condition, or switching agents, unless it's absolutely necessary. Any of these actions simply slows your momentum.

Use Listing Scorecard to Measure Salability

One thing I recommend using is the Listing Scorecard, or Listing Evaluation Form. (See Figure 2, also available at www.jackcotton.com.)

Cape Cod Listing Evaluation Form

| Date | today | | Agent | Jack |

Property | 123 Main Street

Seller | Dewey Listem

List Price | $400,000 | Expiration Date |

Rate the Following:

Seller Motivation

| 1 | 2 | 3 | 4 | 5 | 6 | 7 | 8 | 9 | 10 | **5** |
| No Rush | | | | Neutral | | | | | Wants sold in 30 | |

Condition of Property

| 1 | 2 | 3 | 4 | 5 | 6 | 7 | 8 | 9 | 10 | **6** |
| Poor | | | | Neutral | | | | | Best in Class, Perfect | |

Offering Price in Current Market

| 1 | 2 | 3 | 4 | 5 | 6 | 7 | 8 | 9 | 10 | **6** |
| 10% or more over Market | | | | Neutral | | | | | 3% to 5% | |

Access for Showing

| 1 | 2 | 3 | 4 | 5 | 6 | 7 | 8 | 9 | 10 | **5** |
| 24 Hours Notice | | | | Neutral | | | | | Go & Show | |

Location compared to Competing Offers

| 1 | 2 | 3 | 4 | 5 | 6 | 7 | 8 | 9 | 10 | **7** |
| Inferior | | | | Neutral | | | | | Far Superior | |

Length of Time on Market

| 1 | 2 | 3 | 4 | 5 | 6 | 7 | 8 | 9 | 10 | **9** |
| More than 180 Days | | | | 90 Days | | | | | Less than 30 Days | |

JACK COTTON SPEAKS

Total Score	38
Divide by	/60
Salability Score	63%

90 to 100%	Should sell in 45 days or less if scored honestly.
75 to 89%	Could take as long as 180 days and may need further price adjustment if market changes.
51 to 75%	Need to make adjustments in several areas to increase salability or cancel listing.
50% or less	DO NOT take listing. If already listed, make changes or give back to seller.

Figure 2

This form notes six elements that can affect the length of time it takes to sell your property. You provide a numerical score between 1 and 10 for each of the six elements, which are:

1. Seller's Motivation
2. Condition of the Property
3. Offering Price
4. Access for Showing
5. Location
6. Length of Time on the Market

Seller's Motivation asks this question: "How motivated is the seller? Is the desire to sell only halfhearted?" A desire to sell in the next 30 days would get the highest rating.

Condition of the Property asks the question: "Is the home in perfect show-ready condition?" A pre-inspected home would get the highest rating.

Offering Price asks this question: "Is it comparable and reasonable in the existing market?" An offering price that is 10 percent *less* than the competition would get the highest rating.

Access for Showing should be looked at carefully.

Obviously, the more that access to the property is limited, the more difficult it will be to sell that house. Vacant homes can sometimes get more showings because agents can conduct spur-of-the-moment showings, which may result in a quicker sale and garner the highest rating.

Location asks this question: "How popular is this neighborhood?" If your house is in a great location with few other homes in the area competing with it, then it receives a high score.

The last question to ask is this: "How long has it been on the market?" If it's new on the market—fewer than 30 days—it gets a high score, but if it's been on the market for 180 days or more, the score drops significantly.

At the bottom of the Listing Scorecard, you'll see a place to total the score and divide by 60 to create an average. In the example in Figure 2, the salability score is 63 percent. If the score lands between 51 and 75 percent, it's a sign that adjustments need to be made in several areas to increase the salability of a property. If your rating is below 51 percent, really think about whether you want to sell your home. You might be best served by taking it off the market now and waiting until conditions improve.

Ask Hard Questions

If your goal is to leave no stone unturned in the sale of your house, then that 63 percent needs to come up to at least 90 percent. It's time to go through the scores one at a time, taking an especially close look at the low ones.

Get honest and ask these hard questions:

- How strong is my motivation?
- Do I really want to sell this house?
- If not, should I take it off the market?

You may conclude that, right now, with so many properties available, it doesn't make sense to offer your house if you're not highly motivated.

If you only scored a 6 on the Condition area, what would it take to bring that score up to a 7 or 8? A property in great condition will greatly add to the salability. Again, people look for "best in class" today when investing in property.

Maybe the price needs to be a bit ahead of the market. Perhaps dropping it another five to 10 percent could increase the score to a 7 or 8.

With regard to Access for Showing, perhaps you can dine out more, and hire a cleaning service to come in three days a week. That way, the house can be shown more often—and boost that score up to a 9 or 10.

This Listing Evaluation Form visually quantifies the various stones that shouldn't be left unturned when marketing your property. It lets you clearly see which areas you can tweak to get your score up to 90 percent.

The message is this: If you're serious about getting your property sold, don't do it in a halfhearted, lackadaisical manner. Pull out all the stops and go for it. You'll save time and money in the process.

Action Steps for Secret #11

Go to www.JackCotton.com to download your own copy of the listing scorecard form.

Complete the form for your property.

Think about ways to raise your score looking at the individual items.

Secret #12: Luxury Home Sellers Know Three Rules of Negotiation

Luxury home sellers don't like to feel out-gunned when negotiating the sale of their real estate. After all, these folks close million-dollar deals as part of their everyday activities. Expensive as real estate can be, there is obviously no comparison.

Use Your Market Knowledge

Many first-time home sellers are confused when they set out to place their homes on the market. How much should they sell for?

The answer, of course, is determined on a case-by-case basis. This is why you learn about your target market and study comparables in your neighborhood. Then you mirror luxury home sellers who set prices based on what similar homes with similar usability and utility have sold for, or are currently offered for.

For instance, if you've noticed that several three-bedroom homes in a given area have sold for between $115,000 and $122,000, and you've considered pricing your house at the $130,000 level, you're setting yourself up for a prospective buyer to make an offer that's ten percent off the mark. Keep in mind that market knowledge is your most important ally in negotiating your sale.

Based on everything I've learned over three decades in real estate, these three principles should be your guide to a successful negotiation:

1. Negotiate from a standpoint of self-confidence.
2. Don't assume you know the other party's needs.
3. Detach from the outcome.

Let's look at each point separately.

Negotiate From a Standpoint of Self-Confidence

Self-conficence is a realistic belief in one's own powers: ones abilities, one's judgment; one's capability of rising above a situation or a competitor. If you're self-confident, you're sure you can get the job done, whatever the job might be. As with everything discussed in this book, achieving self-confidence is a process or a journey, not necessarily a destination.

It's been proven that the more self-confident person in a transaction will prevail time and again. Even if you're less-than-stellar in the art of negotiating, a strong measure of self-confidence can carry the day. Much of self-confidence involves a thorough knowledge of your market, and your home's place in it. This takes effort. If you expect to obtain the necessary level of confidence in your knowledge of the market, in four to six weeks, you need to get going—now. You don't want to sit around with a house on your hands realizing you have taken no steps toward the goal of gaining confidence in your knowledge of your marketplace.

I can assure you that most high-end real estate sellers feel confident in their professions. If you have any hope of holding your own, selling homes, achieving and retaining self-confidence must be one of your highest goals.

Don't Assume You Know the Other Party's Needs

The next secret is that high-end sellers assume very little. If one thing can get you into trouble over and over in life, it's making assumptions. When we assume we know the needs of another party, we often take a non-productive course of action.

The result? Your counterparty will dig into a certain position and stay there. Negotiating with someone who's entrenched in that position is often frustrating and fruitless.

The position of a particular buyer may be that he or she will only close in the month of June. In another instance, perhaps the buyer will only offer 70 percent of any asking price.

As soon as a party to a negotiation is stuck at his or her position, the counterparty to the negotiation digs into his or her own position—and the head-butting begins. Stalemate most often results.

In contrast, the luxury real estate seller peels back the layers and looks beyond a certain position to understand the true needs of the parties.

In the example of the closing date needing to be in June, the luxury seller may discover the reason has to do with the shipment date of furniture, art, or antiques. Finding an alternative, yet efficient, means of storing and securing the items before the actual closing date could move the buyer from a dug-in position.

When dealing with a buyer who will only pay a fixed percentage of the asking price, you may be required to peel back more layers. Perhaps this particular buyer is insecure, has high ego needs, or has to get authorization from a third-party trustee. Often, the buyer has a psychological need to look intelligent and capable of negotiating what appears to be (in that buyer's eyes) a great deal. Again, ego.

Once these needs are fully understood, you can provide market evidence as to your perception of the value inherent in this transaction. Perhaps you could present the buyer with data on how much is would cost in your market to build a home like yours. You could offer assessment ratios or other market-based evidence to let this position-based counterparty feel as though he or she has won. For example, if it would cost $200,000 to reproduce your home on a similar lot and the negotiated price has come to $180,000, the buyer would feel like a winner.

In every interaction, both parties to a transaction should find out the other person's "why behind the why" by saying (for example), "Of course, Mr. and Mrs. Buyer, you want to maximize the value of the property you might purchase. Why is it important that you do that in the ways you've specified?" Once you receive this answer from the buyer, go to another level and ask, "What will that do for you and your family? Might there be more than one way for you to meet your goals?"

Only when you truly understand the goals and motivation of the other party can you arrive at creative win-win solutions. If you don't peel back the onion and ask and ask and ask, you may never find the information you need to close the gap.

Based on my experience, people who negotiate from position rather than need often find themselves in stalemate situations—and in a terrible mood. They rarely obtain the outcome they seek.

So it's important to negotiate from need, rather than position, and not assume you know the needs of the counterparty to the negotiation. The seller or agent might tend to assume what the buyer's needs are, based on his or her own beliefs and values.

For instance, if a buyer requests a property that offers complete privacy from neighbors, an agent using his or own belief or value system might assume that the buyer wants a property with five, 10, or more acres. Further probing might lead to the revelation that he or she really wants a special jewel of a property in the part of town where small lots are the norm but are totally contained within walls and year-round landscaping to afford the desired privacy from neighbors. When an agent isn't working with the same definitions that the buyer or seller is, assumptions are frequently incorrect.

One of my first client couples in real estate gave me a laundry list of requirements for the property of their dreams. They wanted an antique "captain's"-type residence, close to the water, on an at least an acre of land. They also wanted high ceilings and a naturally finished wood staircase that would be the focal point of the entry. In addition, they had to have a barn on the property. Based on my conversations with them, all these items seemed exceedingly important.

Then the perfect property finally came on the market and I called them to set up an inspection. I knew from the strange silence at the other end of the phone that something was amiss. It turned out that they had just purchased a house from someone else, in another part of town, that had nothing in common with the description they had given me of their ideal property.

What I had failed to discern in my conversations with them was that while all the needs they'd laid out were indeed important, the *most* important one was getting a great deal. I had not found the "why behind the why."

Although this happened many, many years ago, I still bring it up because this situation still arises frequently. Many buyers have a burning need to tell their friends, relatives, and associates they got the most incredible deal on whatever they just bought. Many times, this usurps what they have laid out in their list of requirements for the new property.

Don't assume you know the needs of the other party *and* don't assume that their needs are exactly as stated.

Detach From the Outcome

The last and most important concept I've learned in negotiating— especially with high-net worth individuals—is to detach from the outcome. If you learn nothing else about negotiating, learn this.

Luxury home sellers let their counterparts to a negotiation know they don't *need* this deal. Whether you're on the selling side or the buying side, always be willing to walk away and realize that sometimes you'll have to. Excessive attachment to the outcome can allow your negotiation process to drift into position-based negotiating rather than need-based negotiating.

Let me explain with an example of how I often present offers to builders of luxury homes. Many builders have high ego needs, making them classic positional negotiators. To make matters more challenging, some builder-sellers want their properties to sell for more money than has ever been realized in the marketplace at any given time.

When an offer did come in on one of my builder listings, the builder's first reaction to the price offer was usually one that I can't put into print here. The negotiation was always position-centered on price. Once egos take over, deals are difficult, if not impossible, to put together.

When I finally learned the concept of detaching from the outcome, it changed my whole approach to presenting offers to this particular builder. When an offer came in (and they were always low because his prices were always high), I'd simply say, "I received an offer on the property at Bay Road." Before the builder-seller could utter a response, I'd say, "I need your authorization to reject the offer." His response always was, "Well, how much is the offer?" I'd say, "It's low, and I need your authorization to reject it. I can't reject offers without your authorization." Then we'd do two or three rounds of this when finally, in frustration, he'd basically scream at me, *"How much is the offer?"*

More often than not, when I stated the amount of the offer, the builder would say, "Well that's not as low as I thought it was based on your presentation. We can work with that." A counteroffer and a different attitude would be forthcoming. The builder was now "saving" a deal, which meant he could save his ego.

Asking for permission to reject the offer before actually disclosing it became the ultimate signal that I was detached from the outcome. I'd demonstrated to this client that I had no expectation of the deal ever coming together. I wasn't trying to push him into accepting something that, while it might have been a good deal, could damage his ego.

n a challenging market where sales can be further apart and fewer in number, the tendency to be attached to the outcome can increase. So more than ever, now is the time to detach from the outcome. High-net-worth individuals can sense weakness just as a thoroughbred horse senses an inexperienced rider or handler.

A close friend of mine who's an attorney has represented many high-end sellers in our market. Once, at a closing, the buyer raised an issue that had come up during the walk-through of the home he was about to purchase. To resolve this issue, he wanted an immediate adjustment of tens of thousands of dollars.

My friend bluntly told the buyer that he should not buy a house with such problems. Then he stood up, packed his briefcase, and began to leave, saying the seller would refund the deposit. He was totally detached from the outcome.

Needless to say, the buyer, his attorney, and the brokers (including me) were all shocked. But within seconds, the buyer was begging my attorney friend to come back, saying he was "only asking. Everything's fine; we'll take the house as is."

Over the years, this exercise was repeated often enough that I always took my time to pack my files, knowing the deal would soon get back on track.

Reach a Favorable Outcome

In each of these three principles of negotiation, understand that your personal power and reputation—as well as that of your counterparty—will enhance your ability to reach a favorable outcome to any particular negotiation.

Your standing or stature in the transaction can't be ignored. Using stature or standing is a favorite tactic of the rich and powerful, likely because it works. For example, who has an easier time negotiating your marketing fee for a particular listing: a former President of the United States or a retired delivery truck driver?

Perception of power, prestige, and standing play a huge role in negotiations. This book is designed to elevate your status to that of a luxury real estate seller. Once you put into practice its ideas and concepts, it will become clear. Not easy, just easier. You may still be out-gunned, you may still be dealing with people who negotiate transactions on a more regular basis than you, but if you follow these principles, you'll have more than a fighting chance.

If a buyer makes an offer on a property that results in numerous counteroffers, you may find your transaction in a position of stalemate. At this point, you might inform the potential buyer that "I will keep looking for another buyer. I'm happy to keep looking; I'm sure another one with a more reasonable offer will come along in the next several months."

Always talk about the market, never talk about position. Often, when a potential buyer sees the chance to get the property begin to slip away, he or she is more willing to compromise.

Ironically, because you've detached from the outcome and are willing to walk away from this transaction, you actually have a better chance of having it go through.

Action Steps for Secret #12

Create a negotiation plan incorporating these tools:

Use market data to determine the best offering price for your home.

Research per-square-foot building costs in your area to determine the replacement cost for your home.

Write out your negotiating points in terms of what's in it for both you and the other party.

Jack Cotton started his real estate company in his college dormitory room 35 years ago and remains active in real estate to this day. Back then, he didn't need to work for another broker to learn the business, because he knew it all at the age of 21. In fact, he knew so much that it took him one year, two months, and three weeks to sell his first house.

Things improved. Over the next three decades, Cotton Real Estate became one of the most admired and professional real estate companies serving buyers and sellers on Cape Cod.

Jack sold Cotton Real Estate to Sotheby's International Realty in 2005. To this day, agents at this firm continue to post the highest per-person sales on the Cape.

Jack focused on growing, running, and managing the firm's Cape Cod offices while still working with high-net-worth clients. Since 2005, he has opened three new offices for Sotheby's International Realty. In the fall of 2008, he stepped down as manager and has returned to being an agent while developing educational products.

Over the years, Jack has been involved in nearly every record-breaking luxury residential sale on Cape Cod, either directly as the agent or as a coach to the agent involved.

His first book, *A Dog's Guide to Life: Lessons from "Moose,"* is in its second printing. Available at most bookstores and Amazon.com, its lessons apply to both the personal and business sides of life.

Other books include:
Selling Luxury Homes
12 Secrets Luxury Home Buyers Know That You Can Use Today

Jack Cotton
851 Main Street
P. O. Box 68
Osterville, MA 02655

508.957.5500
jack@jackcotton.com
www.jackcotton.com

Free Form Downloads

Net Sheet Spreadsheet...........................$35
Listing Evaluation Form.........................$22
Total Value - $57

Download these valuable forms free at www.JackCotton.com
Spreadsheets will be sent to you as an email attachment.

Share Your Story

Starting today, I hope you put the ideas and strategies in this book to use in selling your home.

Send your success stories, home selling ideas, and comments to:

jack@jackcotton.com

You never know, your insights might be included in a future book or program.